THE HEN ARK

Title

The Hen Ark

MARK ROPER

PETERLOO POETS   SALMON PUBLISHING

First published in 1990
by Peterloo Poets
2 Kelly Gardens, Calstock, Cornwall PL18 9SA, U.K.

and
Salmon Publishing
Auburn, Upper Fairhill, Galway, Ireland.

British Library Cataloguing in Publication Data
Roper, Mark
    The hen ark.
    I. Title
    823.914 [F]

   ISBN 1-871471-16-8 Peterloo Poets
       0-948339-47-0 Salmon Publishing

20/3/91

Printed in Great Britain by
Latimer Trend & Company Ltd, Plymouth

ACKNOWLEDGEMENTS are due to the editors of the following journals and anthologies in whose pages some of these poems first appeared: *Belfast Review, Dal gCais* (The Journal of Clare), *Dundalk Poetry Anthology* 1987, *Honest Ulsterman, Irish Press* ('Irish New Writing'), *Poetry Ireland, Poetry Matters, Prospice, The Salmon.*

Eleven of the poems in the present collection appeared in *Peterloo Preview 2* (1990).

This volume was published with assistance from the Ralph Lewis Award at the University of Sussex.

for

Betty Roper and Jane Keen

Contents

Cleaning Ladies

Through the cloisters of the academy
go the round women
brides of the broom
sisters of sweeping
swollen pods of toil

who wait at the pithead
who wait at the docks
who wait by the phone

whose reward is bingo
whose reward is cancer
whose reward is the church

pillars of society
fillers of vacuum
psalters of earth

through the groves of academia
go the swollen girls
moss in their stony wornout wombs
bluebells of smoke in their lungs

who like a bit of sauce
who make ends meet
who go without saying

Birthright

Even as he lifts his blind gum
to her nipple he knows
there is something wrong.

Her mind is elsewhere.
Normal service will not
be resumed. His lips
will close on an absence.

Though she wanted him
so badly, though he seemed
all she could ever want
her lips first closed
on an absence.

She has tried to fill
that hole with this child.
It is almost as simple
as that.

And the voices that gossip
above him are not
celebrating his arrival.
They are making the best,
filling the air, sirens
of a grace that will plague him.

Homesickness for what is
not home, song's bitter sweets,
these ironies enter his soul.

He will not be able
to put this into words.
Others may do so for him
but their words will describe
only as an x-ray describes.

No one can heal
this original hurt.

Someone will pay.
In time he will inherit
no time for his kids.

This is not inevitable.
But it is likely.
This is not unmitigated.
But it is hard.

And all this he knows
as the first slug of milk
trickles into him
and fuels
his necessary cry.

Ann Jackson

'Ann Jackson, born in the City of Waterford of English parents, had several horns growing upon her body.' *Waterford,* Charles Smith (1745).

Her sour breath
reaches down the years
like a wasp
busying through leaves.

'She had not the evacuation
proper to her sex.'
Bureaucracy of blood
sealed off frontiers,

pikestaffed her skin,
shut her up
in a cupboard of bark.

'She spoke but little
and that not plainly.'
What dark tides broke
against the soft lever

of her tongue?
What vixen prowl
obeyed the curfew
of her steepled hide?

'Her eyes looked
very dead.'

Did her mind ride free
on a golden wind
above that pelt of dross?

Maculate conception,
hornchild, scapegoat,

I wish her a fair hearing,
an absence of mirrors,
erosion.

A Woman of Anglo-Ireland

My husband left me without a word,
without a penny. To raise our daughter
I worked nights in a bar, high and dry
in a welter of loosened tongues.

We lived by the river, its lights
furnished our home. At summer's end
we gathered teazles and made them
into toys for sale in town.

I thought we were happy but
she left when she reached sixteen.
I fastened the boreen leaves behind her,
let the river be my only road.

It brings me wood, fattens mussels,
removes my small leavings. I love
its moist kiss in my lungs,
its silver hands between my legs.

You might think I can't cope.
Briars fillet the roof, grease
thickens, books rot, nothing works.

But I stood on the shore with four
dog foxes in a cathedral of moonlight
and they were not afraid of me.

Soft Day

My feet leave no print.
Nothing autographs the air.

Horses plough mist. Looms
of gorse spin scant curtains.

Time stands still. History
happens elsewhere. In a room

of cloud a noise might be
rust shutting rivets on the mind.

I trust nothing. Green skin
conceals a labyrinth of water.

I learn a moorhen's evasivenes,
a snipe's lunatic forbearance.

Parchment damp, razor rusting,
I rehearse retreat to a beehive cell,

the world a dream of soft rain,
the sky a drizzle of angels.

Woodsgift

Nothing registered
on the long thighs
of the mainland
as the ferry slipped out.
I needed no passport
to crawl into this woodwork.
It was child's play.

There are many of us
here, buried alive
in the middle of nowhere.
Safe at last.
Out of reach.

We recognize each other
by one obvious hurt,
our birthmark.
If we talk at all
we steer clear.

In the halflight of peace
only half an ear
registers the hunter's gun,
the chainsaw that eats away
at our cover.

No one gets to perfect
their earthwork, to stick
in the mud forever.
None of us escapes
the salt drag of nativity,
its banal, rivetting wars.

When one finally makes
a break for it
the roadblocks
are already in position.
Beyond them stand
relatives and friends,

anxious to press
their claims.
All that never gave us
a fair start.
All our excuses.

Rise and Fall

a magpie ran a stick
      across morning silence
you lay furled in yourself
      skin warm as rising dough
I got up to make tea
      on the garden clung a frost
so intense I thought
      to see birds hang frozen
in mid-air

      I'll light the fire
bring you tea
      we'll spend a day
in this white cave
      until the light grows
threadbare and majestic
      and unencumbered we slip
into the pool of night
      so deeply pleached
this might be your hair
      these my hands
ourselves a glorious confusion
      unable to tell fruit
from tree

Skindeep

After my bath I put on
your red dressing gown.

It unnerved me. It smelt
so strongly of you.

In a lampshade of flesh
I was haunting, haunted.

Reading Levi you'd asked
if I thought

I could have survived
one of the Camps.

But women were destroyed
immediately and how

should my thin skin survive
the loss of yours?

A vacuum salesman once
drew from our mattress

deposits
of a soft grey talc.

Silt of our spent skins,
mingled, inextricable.

Image of perfect union.
Then he showed us

blown-up photos
of the bugs that thrive

on such leavings.
No phoenix rises

from the rub of two skins
no matter how urgently

how often they kindle
and feast on what lies

between them. The wolf
in sheep's clothing

that spirits one of us
away will leave the other

fleeced, hidebound,
plumbing skindepth.

Cup and Lip

When the towel you threw
knocked my book up
in the air, splashed

coffee everywhere, smashed
my favourite cup
I could have killed you.

But when you bought
me another I thought
if only it were all
so easily replaced:

bowl of thigh, moist eye,
handle of arm, cupped palm

go beyond recall,
are not replaced.

There But For

Chopping firewood a stick
jagged up and scored
my cheek. Another inch
perhaps it would
have pierced my eye.

We are all dead men
on leave, toiling
on high wires,
unable to look the sun
or that fact in the face.

Self-pity thrilled
through me
as I clutched my sad
skull, a moist
christening finger

unfurrowing feature
and care;
as if death were
a going home
through childhood dusk,

the table spread,
the tea strong and hot,
mother cinnamon-spicy
and ginned-up
on forgiveness.

The Cap

I found it in the drawer,
toothpaste smeared, dusty,
its blue container broken.

I checked to see if it was
split, if there was any gap
through which life could enter.

As I held it to the light
they danced in front of me,
the immaculate unconceived,

white-frocked children hurrying
home, singing, calling for
their parents. This is where

the future doesn't come into being.
Our final solution. Our dead end.
Holding it to my ear I hear

the voices of my family
urging me to prolong the line.
'You'd make such a good father'

it insists. Will it divide us
in old age, this ring?
Will we sit together

in a perfectly ordered room,
isolated by this wailing wall,
deafened by its silence?

Easter in Firle Park

It was an Easter of birds,
sparrows at their brawl and bicker,
a thrush on her garden nest,
the first chiffchaff's monotony.

In Firle Park high above the lake
young herons practised patience.
Freed from breeding adults cavorted,
tumbling down the sky with titbits.

We sat on a plastic anorak,
mother and son, a generation.
You were planning to move house,
your final move. You wanted only

a few things around, photos,
a television, some furniture,
grandchildren I do not provide.
Geese busybodied, martins purled

and laced the bright air.
At home we squabbled like lovers
over the washing-up. Chastened
we recoiled, blushing,

the girl shocked from your eyes,
our thoughts frozen
as the stone peacock
we covetted outside the loggia.

Father

I'm trying on your collar
a circlet of white bone

I'm Robin Whitebreast
a whistling in your skin

you're coming clear in me
a five o'clock shadow

at noon: blackmailer,
coalface, you're in my neck

of the woods, your hands
collar my singing throat.

So Shyly, My Parents

In the photograph they lean
together, separated by
an amaryllis hippeastrum
I gave them as a bulb

for Christmas. They smile
shyly, never dreaming
of the cancer hatching
in my father's gut.

They look forward to a long
retirement in which they will
do all the things they don't
have time for just now.

Soon, as he preaches, an abscess
will burst in his stomach.
Its seed will course
his blood and flower.

If it wasn't going to be
a Bank Holiday weekend
he might be spared that increase.
But no such luck and soon

my mother will lean on
an absence which will grow
monstrous as the flower
between their shy smiles.

Yellow and Blue

It was yellow all the way
coming down from the monastery,
euphorbia's sulphur,
hellebore's greengold,
amber beads of fennel,
canary swags of broom,
dusty mustards of flax.

A butterfly ascended
from my father's collection,
a swallowtail resurrected
from those thin drawers
where bodies of air
impaled on rusting pins
lifted threadbare wings.

A ruined tower released
a trickle of goats.
Brass bells splashed
and splintered over
the sun-conjured afternoon.

And then it was blue,
Spanish iris by a pool,
chicory, gentian, comfrey,
the Spanish town drowning
in dusky seashadows,
swallows like thorns
breaking off the bush
of night, like weed
in the wind's tide.

We entered the town.
When I was a child
my father said goodnight to me
in every language he knew.
When I heard the Spanish phrase again
it was like finding birds
ringed by his dead hands.

Swallow Holes

Like so many pegs on a line
hanging a wash of song
they're bunched up on the wires
sensing it's time to be gone.

All summer they've drawn and sheathed
their black blades in the sun.
Lickspittled mud nests to eaves.
Raised their broods of young.

Now some dark instinct orders
through blood or brain or star
their presence on these borders
their passage to Africa.

So the lines stretch clear
across the page, waiting for
the words. Knowing somewhere
they skim and veer through gorge

and gutter, ruin and home,
snatching and greeding
in and out of vase and bone,
mating and breeding.

Until in a moment's grace
they stream through the eye of the pen
and I find pinned to the page
the shadow of their song.

Raw Material

His hand is always in my cupboard.
From the cold storage of his rhyme
I select versions of myself,
garnished to adorn his reflection.

I have found my breasts in a magazine,
my private parts made public knowledge.
In the act of coupling he stays
single, foreign-bodied.

He says it's not the real me
he reproduces. I'm a seed, a figure
of speech. In the same breath
he promises me immortality.

When his scrutiny disfigures,
denatures me he'll stray from
my beaten track, poach in fresh woods,
thought thief, flesh fowler.

But he cannot spare my rib.
He'll come home on my bloodtides,
sing again above my veins,
miraculous in pearling skin. Old age

is a feast I prepare for him.
My last likeness. His swansong.

Charmed Life

Frost fastens
its white irons
on the dwindling days.

At my doorstep
a spilt pincushion
of wrenfeathers.

Thicket-flitter,
eagle-tricker,
fire-bringer.

Chatterbox, lecher,
my Lady of Heaven's hen.
Troglodyte

whose spilt heart
is a thorn in winterside.
In my house now

bloodied milk,
broken bones,
St. Lawrence's fire.

On the altar
of my doorstep
a thimble of ichor,

a host of tiny bones,
a broach of flame
through the dwindling days.

Apricus

In greygreen woods
redroofed houses
curl kittenlike, sunshabby,
husbanding coolness.

Cenobite sunflowers
bend their necks
in drowsy devotion,
drunk with light.

Evening lowers its veils.
Swifts bed the sun
in wreaths of dusk
and dissolving hills.

Across the red earth,
over the sharp cornstalks,
the blackbird night
hatches stars.

I would build a cathedral
of water, the columns
branching fountains,
the crypt a fringed pool,
the nave a dawn lake.

And for the altar
a shock
of dew-pearled wheat.

Harvest

Ancient tribute to fecundity
the harvest show flaunts its trophies.

Stranded on clean butcher's paper
dropsical marrows, ghost fans

of wheat, interminable carrots
trumpet the smug soil's virtue.

At a quiet hoop-la stall
the oldest lady I've ever seen

still plies her trade, in a dress
as faded as a Boer War battle flag.

Few children come to her stall
and they wander away disconcerted

by the terrible determination
with which she moves through her darkness

to collect the hoops, sensing
somehow that they've missed the target.

Sitting, her vague bewildered eyes
search the air, as if it were

full of blows she must avoid.
Death is shadow-boxing with her.

She should have been gathered in long ago.
The routine of the stall is all

that's holding her here now.
Were she once to forget her lines

she would float away,
light and delicate as dandelion seed,

high over apples, beasts and children
into silent soft blue barns.

Soap

On the bathroom sill
our dish of soaps:
jasmine, cucumber, rose.
Gifts, treats, sweet
necessities.

Puritan carbolic,
voluptuous Gallet,
palmolive for pilgrim.
For the jaded Caesar
imperial leather.

My favourite
was cocoa butter.
I kept the empty box
for years, its scent
a chink in time.

Think of it, lawyers
strewing rue across
the floor of chancery
to mask the stench
of poverty;

your grandmother,
goosegreased, sewn
into a vest for winter;
Great War soldiers
crunching lice.

Imagine the soaps
of heaven, astringent
rosemary, healing
feverfew, gentle cubes
of redemption.

Above the Lower Twisted Bones

(The Lower Twisted Bones roughly divide the Olfactory Chamber from the ordinary air passages in the nose. The sense of smell is more acute in the Chamber, which houses the nerves of smell.)

A grain of musk warmed in the palm
will spread its scent half a mile.

After we make love the cat comes
to graze on my musk-sprigged armpits,

as one who would savour the ins
and outs of my performance.

A cat's life is redeemed by floods
of air above the Lower Twisted Bones.

And though we no longer attempt
to nose out the truth, a chance scent

might unleash all the diaries
I never wrote. So when we noticed

how many Roman statues had lost
their noses it seemed no accident

but a deliberate blinding, a bridle
on history, as if somewhere

a hoard of Roman noses held the key
to unknown layers of the Empire.

Fenimore Cooper's 'Deerslayer'

First Prize in the Third Form,
1959, I still haven't read it.
The typeface, tight as dwarf
barbed wire, coldshoulders me.

Cover's split, pages turn to air.
Time to throw it out. Natty
Bumppo, I know you're in there.
So is my bulldozed prep school:

Major Harding, his penchant
for juvenile genitalia
transferred to the cherubim.
Nature Mistress Haslitt,

forcibly taken to the nuthouse,
convinced we'd poisoned her.
And Headmaster Stick, who
melted down the silver cups

and caned us with relish.
A cast of conmen and misfits,
threads in the infinite
unpatterned fluke of my life.

Lest I believe in doctrines,
lest I add theory to my natural
limitations, unread volume,
little red tombstone,
sit tight on the shelf.
Be a token of the random.

Absence of Lilac

Easter Sunday and there's a skin of snow
across the allotments in Birmingham.
I have to cut down an old lilac tree,
so leggy it darkens the garden.

Falling branches splash the Sunday silence.
A vague guilt stirs as sap meets air.
This tree must have seen bombers darken sky
above its first fresh attempts at flower.

My friends doze indoors, tired from a hard night's
nostalgia. I've known them half my life.
Halfway through its span I envy their lives,
their quiet committed union work.

There's a discipline in these parcelled skies.
They'll plant vegetables in earth lit
and freshened by snow and absence of lilac.
The saw poses on the cut trunk.

The scene giddies out of history.
Cocooned in words I bear branches
like standards through the narrow grid
of Midland gardens and hurl them down

onto ashes, broken glass, rusty cans.
My native soil, my own backyard.
As dusk shakes the confidence
of Chamberlain's redbrick city I go

in to the warmth, wake my friends.
We head for the pub. Through the blurry mirth
continually comes the image
of a cut stump struggling to escape its ground.

After Lazarus

Below snail shell
and small bird remains,
below worm galleries

and the tusked roots
of trees, past stones
like Lazarus never dreaming

to see sun again, past
all feature and relic
a remembered place.

Rest your spade.
Stars seed
a steady dark.

Rest in the pulse
of unnamed water
rising to light.

Loose nightwinds
fall like scarves
across your shoulders.

Now mammoth and elk
come to the edge
of the clearing.

Now peat recites
a litany of leaf,
opens bibles of bark.

The tip of your spade
is greening, branching.

Harristown Dolmen

We came in pale hawthorn light.
More cats than people patrolled

the roads. A horse pissed
in shadow. Haycocks were breasts

without nipples. The stones sprung
at the junction of three fields.

You said music raised them.
I said people lifted them,

inch by ton-defiant inch
people were forced to lift

this stone ear this stone vase
into which out of which pour

the nightingales of water,
the honeysuckle sweet nothings

of speech, the sweat and silence
of those who suffer and those

who build on their suffering.

Lindisfarne

The photo shows us gathering mussels
on the foreshore. After we ate them
you and I quarrelled, a row fought
between bouts of violent retching.

Downstairs Bart annotated Muir.
We had the cottage for a week,
walked round and round the island,
drank gallons of Old Peculier but never

got drunk. Most nights we watched T.V.
but once we raced barefoot across
an icy incoming tide, sharp shells
cutting an ecstasy into our feet.

None of you knew how I slipped out
to stand under the statue of Aidan,
its peace a disturbance I craved.
Cast up thirteen hundred years

from the agony of flesh he outstares
the passionate sea. Above him the ruined
chancel window sustains its arch,
a stone rainbow in the northern sky.

Away From It All

I often pick them up
hitching from the ferry,
backpackers trying to reach
the West before nightfall.

Teenage Dutch or German, here
to get away from it all,
in vacant speechless greenery
away from Europe. We watch

light shrink in the river,
praise the smell of grass,
the fat cattle making milk,
the lack of industry.

I drop them off by
the small petrol station,
its young owner just dead
from a heart attack.

Their road runs on by
the khaki river, rank
with effluent from field
and factory and sometimes

the bodies of others
who wanted to get away.
I head slowly back
to my small square of land,

past broken-egg cottages
and a castle full of sky.
In the few remaining elms
rooks broadcast their control.

The Old Apple Orchard

The apple engine
no longer works.
Branches have fused.
No blossom oils
their snarl-up.

Bullfinches haunt
a choked lung,
a carcass
which incubates
a flash-fire.

The grass is sour,
flowerless.
Tears of lichen
turn to dust.

The child that played here
would be frightened.

The trees have such
a terrible grip
on one another.

An Act of Union

As a child I was terrified
of Heaven so when you told me
we were two precious souls
I was less than impressed.

We never did have sex
in that high house though
light and hope rained
on the tired walls and we held

each other's spines, instruments
we thought we might learn
to play. I remembered
a body on a rubbish dump,

skinned spine jutting from
a pair of trousered legs.
Such heart searching!
Such unobtainable revenge!

We agreed our differences
were settled, reserving
my right to be reserved,
your right to a dictionary

that turned all words
to love or mist. In the park
a beech tree swallowed
its fugitive gleam.

From each amputated bough
swung the ghost of a chance.
We shook hands and left
in our separate cars.

Nightwalk Abroad

In the dark, from a distance, the lit cottage
was a star, the last in a constellation fallen

onto the hill at whose feet I have come to live.
The closer I came to the window's brand

the more hostile it appeared, as if accusing
my foreign body, questioning its right of passage.

The cottage shifted in its stall, cats humped
like giant tics on a windowsill. It saw

through me and I was glad to escape its orbit.
I was taking the air, letting the wind fondle

the twigs of my hair, letting it reel through
the branches of my ears. I'd taken the precaution

of wearing my fluorescent Savings Bank armband
and indeed I was a priceless asset as I climbed

to the top of the hill where the Plough dipped
its crooked scoop into thin air. The constellation

of rooted lights behind me seemed as remote
as that Plough. But the rinse of starlight woke

its ghosts, loosened histories like hair.
Cottages abandoned and ruined, language silenced,

a dark circuit of hunger and oppression,
bitter memories and hatred for my kind.

The White Lady's Tree

'In 1649 Cromwell gave Sir John Ponsonby the house of the Daltons, Kidalton. Sir John kept Dalton and his family on as guests. It appeared he would marry Dalton's daughter Cathy, until one day he returned with a lady whom he introduced as his wife. Cathy collapsed in a fit and never recovered her sanity.'

What could I do but act mad?
He brought another woman into
my house when he had promised
to marry me. All night I danced
in red hot shoes, my fingers
mocked me with absence of rings.

But by day I had to appear
in their company. I wore
my white wedding dress, became
the lily of my grief, a cold
flower in the church of their love.

I sat in an old thorn tree
with a scissors, snipping tips
and buds from the young branches.
They thought me quite insane.
I fell into a swoon and died
on my father's grave.

My ghost sat on in the white
lady's tree and spied on generations
of their coupling, until at last
the house was burnt down. Years
after, one of them returned, looking
for the grave of a child.

When he found the stone he took
a packet of mixed flower seed
from his wallet and shook it out
on the grass. Wind and mice
feasted that night. And that's all
there is. Soon only the trees
will remember his coming.

Body Number 115

'the body of a man burnt to death in the King's Cross Fire of November 1987, which could not be identified.'

Perhaps you wandered down
for a bit of warmth,
to rub against someone,
to lose yourself in a crowd.

Or you hurried down
cold and deliberate
into that forest of flesh,
to undergo its indifference,
to whet your contempt.

Already you had travelled
far beyond all networks
of love, were beyond
recognition even then.

Fire sealed your incognito,
perfected your alibi
but you were not suffered
to remain in the underworld.
Isolation ended here,
in a blaze of publicity.

What we choose to call
your identity entered
the official imagination
and stuck.

You were taken apart.
Bits of you parcelled up
and passed around the kingdom
like glass slippers.

Hands offered a fingerprint.
Teeth a set of initials.
Brain a specialized clip.

They fitted no one.
Nothing put you together again.
Would you have recognized
the poster's reconstructed face?

There was no shortage
of claimants,
so many people looking
for someone they'd lost,
someone they did
or didn't want back.

You were not their man.
Filing cabinets multiply.
What's left of you
lingers in a mortuary
with other unidentified
remains, on the edge
of the other world.

There may never be
a world so perfect
that all the coldshouldered
might be taught
to love themselves again.

But somewhere there is a name
for you, a history
that fits only you,
a human print that lacks you.

And somewhere there must be
water for you,
burnt offering of negligence,
a place where you might
peel off the black disguise
and show your face.

Until then your body hangs
in the wardrobe of those
who saved their skins.

Anonym, Darkhorse, Loveless,
you fell through all systems
of knowing as surely
as a cigarette fell
through an escalator.

You buried yourself
as surely as dust
and grease were left
collect on the machines.

You couldn't quite
extinguish yourself,
leaving the meteorite
of your body
and its unknown provenance
and the great hole it leaves
in our atmosphere.

The Boat Women

She is crossing the sea
with the germ of a child
she does not want to bear.

It will not register
at Customs: the soft load
presses most on her mind.

There is no ritual
for this: the decision
to stay single, the end

of a possible life.
She has studied pictures
of embryos, the size

of safety pins, human.
She is not in the dark.
There will always remain

guilt, a scar, flawed tissue
where a branch didn't grow.
She will come home having

lost a little weight, gained
a little quiet around
her heart. Her grief can't be

made public: illegal,
this complex compromise,
this human choice, to be

swept under the carpet.
Here are weeping mothers,
children no one wanted,

women worn to the bone.
She chose not to increase.
She has stayed in one piece.

Her body is her own.

True North

Lately the drive home
seems to take longer.
Air is less predictable.
Seasons touch extremes.

At dawn birds recite
the news, reports
of cars that run on silence,
knees that cap themselves.

It seems our lives
are running off the map.
Frightened by obscure
threat in rook-cackle

I come home to your bed.
I know by heart
the overture of your undress,
its modest concealments,

its sudden revelations.
I go blindfold
through the land of your flesh,
its contours firm beneath me.

I shoot the sun
by these nutbrown moles,
my true north
this constellation of freckle.

Firelight

I'd light the fire without meaning to,
I'd light it without noticing,
kindling and coal using my hands
to combust on the very warmest of days.

You in the light green chair, I in
the dark green we'd sit, fire
flowering between us, its black nightgowns
slipping to the floor. Already

memorable, the coal that burnt
re-deposited within us,
a mine of ripeness, seam of grace.
Where unknown others sat before

and unknown others will again
we'd take our time. Fire privy
to our intimacies, fire
privy to the unspoken questions:

What is the price of seclusion?
What have we missed, being childless?
Its mild blast on our skin always
a reminder, a hint of a darkness

burnt into human skin in suburbs far
from an explosion. Mask of Hiroshima,
shadow scorched into all our flesh.
Good servant, bad master fire insists.

Last thing we'd lie awake and watch
dying flames infiltrate the bedroom
and dapple the walls. We'd hear
the soft toc as clinker hit the pan.

A sudden flare might send me stumbling out
to check all was well. I'd hurry
back, sobered, in violation
of a privacy. To see the fire gently

collapsing, talking to itself, heating
empty chairs, was to know what
the world would look like when
we're not there. Was to be thin air.

Flying the Coop

The boy roosts in the coop,
his skin thickening
in wing-spanned air.
The old birds moan on
about routine flights,
the need for food,
a ring of feathers where
a friend had been.

The boy knows it will be
different for him.
Ahead lie the miles,
the unfenced empire of air.
It's all his and he will
never be so pure again,
coming to consciousness
in a soft controlled
explosion of feathers.

He watches an adult roll
an egg across the rough floor,
away from the cage
it was removed to,
where black is bred
with black and red
eliminated.

He tries his raw wings.
No one has designs on him.
He is so safe
in this applause of feathers,
this endless forgiveness
of air.

How could he know these are
the adults he must mock
and conquer, only to imitate
helplessly. That he lies
in a nest he must build
again and defend.
That he carries the coop
inside himself.

In the Choir Stall

The choir vestry smelt of fart
and polish. You could hide
in the cupboard but the smell

would find you. The cassocks
had sweat-yellowed armpits,
odd buttons, torn linings.

We hid them under starch white
surplices, thin tin medallions
on coloured strings. Shoes

and faces betrayed us. I was
10 when Miss Blackstone keeled
over dead at matins. They locked

her spinster body in the vestry
until an ambulance could come.
I found the key and slipped in,

circled this object both there
and not there, losing its heat
on the gritty carpet. Her shoes

protruded. I wanted to lift
the cloth over her face but
was afraid she would look, afraid

she would not look. At evensong
the cry rose in my throat,
my days, like the hymns, numbered.

Winter Visitors

The current that reels
between us on our Christmas
family walk still startles.

The snow-strung wind
that stings our faces
cannot dull our spites.

Mother walks on ahead
too old to settle
our grievances.

We are the adults now,
fencing with mortgages
and pre-menstrual tension.

The city silvers the valley.
Married selves wait
for us, cars, careers,

bank balancing acts.
A chill mud clings.
Migrant fieldfare

snatch the last berries
from stunted hawthorn.
For the festive season

we are winter visitors,
sensing familiar blood
through sheets of snow.

No Country for Old Men

There they understand that most
men's lives are finished by thirty.
They round them up into flocks,
allow them to roam and reminisce.

There is little dissent. The men
demand uniforms, rules, officers
whom they serve with a canine
compassion. Mornings are

the worst time. Regret hangs
tangible as rivermist and eyes
staring down the past are like
a blank cathedral window. Otherwise

they make themselves useful,
grow attached to the silence
in plants and pipes, perform
their duties without question.

Of their sex lives little
is known. One of their banners
unfurled displays a pattern
of limp penises, all faced

out of their soft nests in the one
direction, waiting for no tide,
strangely defeated. They are
kept apart from young men

and they bury their own. Mourning
consists of endless distracted
sighs. It is rumoured
their sad eyes are bottomless.

The Coroner

A corpse is an envelope.
He whips it open, rummages
for trinket of cyst or tumour.

He never catches the last
thing on your mind. He wants
the body's reason to quit,

its hidden need to drop
all you thought it stood for
and let thought perish.

No one leaves without
a certificate. Detective
of inadvertent departure

he breaks and enters
with drill and power saw,
ignores frayed nerves

to stand immune in wellingtons
among the echoes of fever,
the catacombs of cancer,

the stalled unstartable hearts.
He redeems nothing but will
offer an ersatz eternity.

A stitched up smile, touched
up cheeks, a weight
off your mind: you'll never

look so well, a picture
of health to hang in the air
as the credits roll.

Hair Peace

When reading you used
catch, twist, lick
a strand of hair.

You'd place it gently
in your ear, until
it grew quite cold.

A circuit was completed,
a bright halo which
left me in the dark.

Now you've had your hair
cut short, your hands
flutter like moths

at the lamp of your ear.
I've made a ring
of hair.

It's a betrothal.
Try it for size.
It binds you to nothing.

Pollinators

Some pollinators don't give
a rap for colour

so there's no point in the flower
which needs their services

laying on a colourful display.
It had better waft a putrid stench

to bring on the bluebottles
as do members of the arum family

or else imitate the appearance
of the pollinator itself

as do the bee and fly orchids.
All day the sun beats

on warm breastshadows, on thighs
cocked like guns. I hurry home

as if drawn through the soft-tongued
throats of many flowers,

golden-dusted, musky;
led irresistibly where

the pale fields of your stomach
slope to black brambled wildness.

The Hen Ark

The horse broke your heart,
one day knocked you
unconscious, made your life

unbearable. You'd had
enough of animal husbandry
but in the uncovenanted grace

of this Indian summer
sun gilds hexagons of wire
on a homemade hen ark.

You busy with scraps, armfuls
of feathery straw, divining
differences between

our six pullets. Through
cluck and chirr one comb
raddles and swells. Tonight

you bring the first egg,
its shell naive and flawless
as your smile. Later

we crack it on a cup:
two gold yolks
in a wedding gown of albumen.